THE PROCESS

STUDY GUIDE

The Process
The Journey Between God's Promises Received and Fulfilled

Copyright © 2023 Mattheus van der Steen

Published by Arrows & Stones

Author: Mattheus van der Steen
Editor: Hope Visser
Cover design: Glenn van der Mull
Interior design: Ronald Gabrielsen, 3ig.org

ISBN 978-1-960678-80-5

All Scripture quotations are taken from the THE HOLY BIBLE, NEW INTERNATIONAL VERSION®. Copyright © 1973, 1978, 1984, 2011 by Biblica, Inc.™. Used by permission of Zondervan.

The spelling of tetragrammaton and the use of honorific capitals has been changed to match the publisher's house style of this book. Italicization of Bible texts has been added by the author.

For the sake of readability, inclusive language such as "he" or "she" and "his" or "her" has been abandoned, and the pronouns "he" and "his" have been chosen as neuter terms.

All rights reserved. No portion of this book may be reproduced, stored in a retrieval system or transmitted in any form, electronically, mechanically, by means of photocopying, recording or otherwise—with the exception of brief quotation in printed reviews—without the prior permission of the publisher.

THE PROCESS

MATTHEUS VAN DER STEEN

STUDY GUIDE

ARROWS &
STONES

CONTENTS

Chapter 1. You Have a Promise 6

Chapter 2. The Process 10

Chapter 3. Storms 14

Chapter 4. Self-inflicted Storms 18

Chapter 5. Demonic Storms 22

Chapter 6. God Storms and the Pitfall of Rejection 28

Chapter 7. Hope Is the Key 32

Chapter 8. Perfect Storm 36

Chapter 9. How to Keep on Going 40

Chapter 10. Fulfillment of the Promise 46

FOREWORD BY **BILL JOHNSON**

THE PROCESS

THE JOURNEY BETWEEN
GOD'S PROMISES RECEIVED
AND FULFILLED

**MATTHEUS
VAN DER STEEN**

CHAPTER 1

YOU HAVE A PROMISE

There is a season in which all the promises of God are fulfilled.

READING TIME

As you read Chapter 1: "You Have a Promise" in *The Process*, review, reflect on, and respond to the text by answering the following questions.

REVIEW, REFLECT, AND RESPOND

What promises have you received? How have they been fulfilled?

_____
_____
_____
_____
_____
_____

Do you ever find it difficult to be patient while waiting for your promise? Why or why not?

_____
_____
_____
_____
_____
_____

What do you do while waiting for your promise? Are you thankful in the meantime? How do you remain in God's presence?

_____
_____
_____
_____
_____
_____

> *Timothy, my son, I am giving you this command in keeping with the prophecies once made about you, so that by recalling them you may fight the battle well, holding on to faith and a good conscience....*
>
> —*1 Timothy 1:18-19a*

Consider the scripture above and answer the following questions:

What promises can you recall in the midst of battle, like Timothy?

_____
_____
_____
_____
_____
_____
_____
_____

When you receive a promise, do you believe, speak it out, and act on it, or do you keep it to yourself? Explain your answer.

_____
_____
_____
_____
_____
_____
_____
_____
_____

In what way are you a part of a Christian community? How does this community help you?

_____
_____
_____
_____
_____
_____
_____
_____
_____
_____

How do you stay focused on God and His promises? Are you willing to undergo the process—and all it entails—to see His promises actualized?

_____
_____
_____
_____
_____
_____
_____
_____
_____
_____

CHAPTER 2

THE PROCESS

Transition is a process in which our soul becomes more like the finished work of Jesus.

READING TIME

As you read Chapter 2: "The Process" in The Process, review, reflect on, and respond to the text by answering the following questions.

REVIEW, REFLECT, AND RESPOND

In your own words, what is a transition?

_____
_____
_____
_____
_____
_____
_____
_____
_____
_____

What is a recent transition you went through? How did it make you feel?

_____
_____
_____
_____
_____
_____
_____
_____
_____
_____
_____

Have you ever been discouraged or felt like giving up during a transition? If so, what caused this?

_____
_____
_____
_____
_____
_____
_____
_____

What is the "Bible school bubble"? Why is this dangerous?

_____
_____
_____
_____
_____
_____
_____
_____

How strong would you say your spiritual muscles are on a scale of 1-10? Are you content with this number? What can you do to increase it?

1   2   3   4   5   6   7   8   9   10

_____
_____

What are you going through right now? What do you think God is trying to teach you, and how do you think He is trying to grow you?

Are you willing to undergo the process, even if there are storms and obstacles present along the way? Why?

CHAPTER 3

STORMS

*The heroes of faith needed the storm
in order to reach their destiny.*

READING TIME

As you read Chapter 3: "Storms" in The Process, review, reflect on, and respond to the text by answering the following questions.

REVIEW, REFLECT, AND RESPOND

What storm have you undergone recently?

_____
_____
_____
_____
_____

Think of a storm from your past. What did you learn from this experience? How did you grow?

_____
_____
_____
_____
_____
_____

In what way are storms necessary for the process? Is there any way around them?

_____
_____
_____
_____
_____
_____

> *And I tell you that you are Peter, and on this rock I will build my church, and the gates of Hades will not overcome it.*
>
> —Matthew 16:18

Consider the scripture above and answer the following questions:

What is the significance of what Jesus said in this verse? What kind of opposition can you expect?

_____
_____
_____
_____
_____
_____
_____

What storm-related lesson can we learn from cows and buffalo? How does this apply practically to your life?

_____
_____
_____
_____
_____
_____
_____
_____
_____

What part of us are affected by the storms we encounter?

___

Whom are you surrounding yourself with, and whom are you letting speak into your life? Are there any influences you know should not be there?

___

Have you ever let your emotions lead your decision-making? How did things turn out? What did you learn?

___

CHAPTER 4

SELF-INFLICTED STORMS

Some storms are caused by wrong decision or sin.

READING TIME

As you read Chapter 4: "Self-Inflicted Storms" in The Process, review, reflect on, and respond to the text by answering the following questions.

REVIEW, REFLECT, AND RESPOND

What is a self-inflicted storm? How can you guard against this type of storm?

_____
_____
_____
_____
_____
_____
_____
_____
_____
_____

Have you ever experienced a self-inflicted storm? What happened? What did you learn?

_____
_____
_____
_____
_____
_____
_____
_____
_____
_____
_____

What sin did King David commit in 2 Samuel 11 that led to a self-inflicted storm? Have you ever tried to conceal your storm like David?

_____
_____
_____
_____
_____
_____

> *David was greatly distressed because the men were talking of stoning him; each one was bitter in spirit because of his sons and daughters. But David found strength in the LORD his God.*
>
> *—1 Samuel 30:6*

Consider the scripture above and answer the following questions:

What does it mean to find strength in the Lord?

_____
_____
_____
_____
_____
_____
_____

When have you gone to the Lord to find strength in the middle of a storm?

_____
_____
_____
_____

How do you calm a self-inflicted storm?

What past wrongs do you need to take responsibility for and repent for?

Are you offended easily? Why? What are the dangers of being offended?

CHAPTER 5

DEMONIC STORMS

Asking God for the keys to breakthrough will bring victory.

READING TIME

As you read Chapter 5: "Demonic Storms" in *The Process*, review, reflect on, and respond to the text by answering the following questions.

REVIEW, REFLECT, AND RESPOND

Have you ever experienced a demonic storm? How did you respond? What was the outcome?

_____
_____
_____
_____
_____
_____
_____
_____
_____
_____

What do you think of the demonic storm Job experienced? Would you have reacted in the same way Job did? In what ways?

_____
_____
_____
_____
_____
_____
_____
_____
_____

Have negative influences ever tried to speak into your life in the midst of your storm? What did they say? Did you listen?

_____
_____
_____
_____
_____
_____
_____
_____

> *Therefore put on the full armor of God, so that when the day of evil comes, you may be able to stand your ground, and after you have done everything, to stand.*
>
> *—Ephesians 6:13*

Consider the scripture above and answer the following questions:

What is the armor of God? How do you attain it?

_____
_____
_____
_____
_____
_____
_____
_____

Is this the only way to resist attacks from the enemy? Why or why not?

_____
_____
_____
_____
_____
_____
_____
_____
_____
_____

How do you attain the keys to break through and conquer the storm? Is there only one way of doing this?

_____
_____
_____
_____
_____
_____
_____
_____
_____
_____

Have your storms ever turned into blessings? If so, how? Write about the situation.

_____
_____
_____
_____
_____
_____
_____
_____
_____
_____

How did Jesus deal with demonic opposition in Mark 4-5? Why do you think He responded this way?

_____
_____
_____
_____
_____
_____
_____
_____
_____
_____

Do you think it is possible for us to respond to demonic storms as Jesus did in your previous answer? Why or why not?

_____
_____
_____
_____
_____
_____
_____
_____
_____
_____

Are storms avoidable if we want to gain new territory for God's kingdom? Why?

_____
_____
_____
_____
_____
_____
_____
_____
_____
_____

CHAPTER 6

GOD STORMS AND THE PITFALL OF REJECTION

You will never discover the open door of your promise until you have dealt with the closed doors in your life.

READING TIME

As you read Chapter 6: "God Storms and the Pitfall of Rejection" in *The Process*, review, reflect on, and respond to the text by answering the following questions.

REVIEW, REFLECT, AND RESPOND

Have you ever experienced a God storm? How did this storm make you feel: Confused? Betrayed? Rejected?

_____
_____
_____
_____
_____
_____
_____
_____
_____

Why do you think God sends storms our way? How do they effectively teach us?

_____
_____
_____
_____
_____
_____
_____
_____
_____

> *Then Jesus was led by the Spirit into the wilderness to be tempted by the devil.*
>
> —*Matthew 4:1*

Consider the scripture above and answer the following questions:

What stands out to you from this verse?

_____
_____
_____
_____
_____
_____
_____

Why do you think the Spirit led Jesus to be tempted? What was the purpose of this?

_____
_____
_____
_____
_____
_____
_____

When does a God storm end? What will help us in the midst of the storm?

_____
_____
_____

Have you ever tried to solve your God storm with something that was not the solution? Describe the experience.

When have you experienced rejection? How did it make you feel?

What opportunities arose from the above rejection?

CHAPTER 7

HOPE IS THE KEY

If you don't know how to navigate through rejection, you will end up going in circles.

READING TIME

As you read Chapter 7: "Hope Is the Key" in *The Process*, review, reflect on, and respond to the text by answering the following questions.

REVIEW, REFLECT, AND RESPOND

What mindset do you want to have in the middle of your future storms? How does this differ from your current mindset?

_____
_____
_____
_____
_____
_____
_____
_____
_____
_____

How do you want to deal with rejection? How can you remain grateful despite being rejected?

_____
_____
_____
_____
_____
_____
_____
_____
_____
_____

When did Jesus experience rejection? How did He respond?

_____
_____
_____
_____
_____
_____
_____
_____
_____
_____
_____
_____

When have you experienced betrayal? How did you react? Explain the situation.

_____
_____
_____
_____
_____
_____
_____
_____
_____
_____
_____
_____

How can you remain hopeful in the midst of life's storms?

What rejection have you experienced recently? Where did this rejection point you?

CHAPTER 8

PERFECT STORM

A perfect storm often affects your family, friends, and the ministry or church connected to you.

READING TIME

As you read Chapter 8: "Perfect Storm" in *The Process*, review, reflect on, and respond to the text by answering the following questions.

REVIEW, REFLECT, AND RESPOND

In your own words, what is a "perfect storm"?

_____
_____
_____
_____
_____
_____
_____
_____
_____
_____

Have you ever experienced a perfect storm? What was it? How did you overcome it, or are you still working to overcome it?

_____
_____
_____
_____
_____
_____
_____
_____
_____
_____

If you have experienced a perfect storm, what were your emotions?

_____
_____
_____
_____
_____
_____
_____
_____
_____
_____
_____

> *Jesus said, "Father, forgive them, for they do not know what they are doing." And they divided up his clothes by casting lots.*
>
> *—Luke 23:34*

Consider the scripture above and answer the following questions:

How did Jesus respond when faced with His "perfect storm"?

_____
_____
_____
_____
_____
_____
_____
_____
_____

When has anyone attacked you or gossiped about you? Did you blame them or the spirit behind them? How can you tell?

_____
_____
_____
_____
_____
_____
_____
_____

What is the significance of the Leviathan?

_____
_____
_____
_____
_____
_____
_____
_____

What does the Word say about how can we slay the Leviathan?

_____
_____
_____
_____
_____
_____
_____
_____

CHAPTER 9

HOW TO KEEP ON GOING

*Learn to trust God's Spirit to lead
you through the thick fog.*

READING TIME

As you read Chapter 9: "How to Keep on Going" in *The Process*, review, reflect on, and respond to the text by answering the following questions.

REVIEW, REFLECT, AND RESPOND

When have you had to trust God amidst "thick fog"? How did you trust Him?

_____
_____
_____
_____
_____
_____
_____
_____
_____
_____
_____

How do you draw nearer to God each day? What more could you possibly do?

_____
_____
_____
_____
_____
_____
_____
_____
_____
_____

Do you only draw nearer to God when you need to overcome a storm? Explain your answer.

_____
_____
_____
_____
_____
_____
_____
_____

> *The LORD is my shepherd, I lack nothing. He makes me lie down in green pastures, he leads me beside quiet waters, he refreshes my soul. He guides me along the right paths for his name's sake.*
>
> *—Psalm 23:1-3*

Consider the scripture above and answer the following questions:

How does this passage make you feel?

_____
_____
_____
_____
_____
_____
_____
_____
_____

How do you look at the Lord as your shepherd? What does this entail?

_____
_____
_____
_____
_____
_____
_____
_____
_____
_____
_____
_____
_____

When has God sent you someone or something to help you in the midst of your storm? What or who was it? How were you helped?

_____
_____
_____
_____
_____
_____
_____
_____
_____
_____
_____
_____

How do you take care of yourself? Do you feel like you focus enough on self-care?

_____
_____
_____
_____
_____
_____
_____
_____
_____
_____
_____

Whom do you have in your life to hold you accountable for your actions? Why them?

_____
_____
_____
_____
_____
_____
_____
_____
_____
_____
_____

What kind of favor follows the storm? What kind of favor do you think waits on the other side of your storm?

_____
_____
_____
_____
_____
_____
_____
_____
_____
_____
_____
_____
_____

CHAPTER 10

FULFILLMENT OF THE PROMISE

Don't make your healing conditional on your validation.

READING TIME

As you read Chapter 10: "Fulfillment of the Promise" in *The Process*, review, reflect on, and respond to the text by answering the following questions.

REVIEW, REFLECT, AND RESPOND

Which of the four seasons of life are you currently in?

_____
_____
_____
_____
_____
_____
_____
_____
_____
_____

How can you prepare for the next step of the process?

_____
_____
_____
_____
_____
_____
_____
_____
_____
_____
_____

What stands out to you about Joseph's promise?

___

> *"For I know the plans I have for you," declares the LORD, "plans to prosper you and not to harm you, plans to give you a hope and a future."*
>
> *—Jeremiah 29:11*

Consider the scripture above and answer the following questions:

Do you believe that God has unique plans for your life? What kind?

___

What were the different ways in which Joseph was tested? How are you being tested today?

_____
_____
_____
_____
_____
_____
_____
_____
_____
_____
_____
_____

How might your pride be blocking your blessing? How do you keep your pride in check?

_____
_____
_____
_____
_____
_____
_____
_____
_____
_____
_____
_____

What practical takeaway from this study guide can you apply to your life immediately?

_____
_____
_____
_____
_____
_____
_____
_____
_____
_____
_____
_____

www.ingramcontent.com/pod-product-compliance
Lightning Source LLC
Chambersburg PA
CBHW072011090426
42734CB00033B/2494